Jason
The "Jj" Juggler

Jason

Jason

Jason

Written By

Fannie Lewis Barnes

Illustrated By

Gaurav Bhatnagar

This book is the property of:

To: _____

From: _____

Date: _____

Message:

ISBN: 978-1-7376571-8-7

Printed – United States of America

Dedication Page

This book is dedicated to our son, Jason. He is and has been a Blessing to us as a "Great Son" and an "Inspiring Supporter!"

Therefore, I find it only befitting to devote this book to him due to his past enjoyment and love for listening to the reading of children stories during his early learning years.
Love you and God Bless!!!!

J – Joyful
A – Awesome
S – Supporter
O – Optimistic
N – Nice

As always, I want to thank my family for their continued love and support in my writing endeavors.

R	E	A	D
R	E	A	D
e	n	n	e
l	j	d	v
a	o		e
x	y		l
			o
			p

The first part of this book is about how Jason, the "Jj" Juggler enjoys juggling various things as long as they begin with the letter, "Jj."

The latter part of this book introduces a communication method with permission, via the American Society for Deaf Children. This method is the American Sign Language (ASL) Alphabet and Numbers Charts.

The goals are for scholars to:
1. Understand the importance of being able to communicate with the hard of hearing and the deaf population.

2. Awaken another part of the hearing population's cognitive mindset into learning this unique method of communication.

Learn To Read

L ~ listen
E ~ explore
A ~ absorb
R ~ remember
N ~ notice

T ~ try
O ~ observe

R ~ respond
E ~ enjoy
A ~ accomplish
D ~ discover

R E A D

Relax with this little book
Enjoy it from the shelf,
And you will see that you can
Develop skills all by yourself!

J – Juggling
A – Another
S – Skillful
O – Original
N – Narrative

Words to Know

jelly

January

jeans

juggler

July

jacket

June

jello

juice

jam

4

Jason, the "Jj" Juggler

Jason really likes the letter "Jj,"
he will not have it any other way.

Some "Jj" things are easy for him,
this is why he juggles them.

To him the "Jj's" are not a struggle,
he'll tell of things he likes to juggle.

"First of all, I want to say,
that my first name begins with J."

"Jason, the Juggler is my name,
can you juggle these things the same?"

"Readers listen to what I say,
here are my favorites that begin with Jj."

"Jason the juggler is who I am,
I like to juggle these jars of jam."

"If you don't want jam in your belly,
watch as I juggle these jars of jelly."

"Since I do not have jelly beans,
I will juggle these blue jeans."

"I do not juggle tennis rackets,
but I will juggle these green jackets."

"I'll juggle the first month, January,
as you locate it in your dictionary."

January

January

January

"I can also whistle a happy tune,
as I juggle the sixth month, June."

June

June

June

"I will not juggle this one too high,
the seventh month which is July."

July

July

July

"I dare not juggle a train or caboose,
but I will juggle this juicy juice."

13

"Royal readers, I am glad you came,
to watch me juggle my first name."

Jason

Jason

Jason

"Fabulous friends before I go,
I will juggle these boxes of jello."

"I will juggle things during the day,
as long as they begin with the letter, Jj!"

"Well loyal learners, my part is done, so
long for now from Juggling Jason!"

"Royal readers before you go play,
say these new words that begin with Jj!"

"Learn these "Jj" words at your own pace,
some are upper and some are lower case."

jet	Jason	jeep
Jonnie	just	Jupiter
jump	Joe	jug
jingle	jaw	Joyce

Now, fabulous friends, the juggler is done, but he wants you to become skilled while you're having fun!

The latter pages that you will find, are all prepared with you in mind.

They are included, I must confess, to assess your skills and cognitive awareness!

Various activities, worksheets and tasks, are provided for you and you didn't have to ask!

So listeners and scholars, work until the end, and show your guide that you did comprehend!

Activity Sheet

Draw lines to match the same words

jam	jeans
jello	juggler
January	June
juice	jam
jacket	July
jeans	January
jelly	jello
June	jacket
July	jelly
juggler	juice

Activity Sheet

Write the same word on the line next to it

January _____

jam _____

juice _____

jacket _____

jello _____

July _____

juggler _____

jelly _____

jeans _____

June _____

Activity Sheet

Fill in the blanks with the correct letters

jello	___ e l l o
July	J ___ ___ y
jacket	j a ___ k e ___
juice	___ u ___ c ___
jam	j ___ m
jeans	___ e ___ n ___
juggler	j ___ g ___ l ___ r
jelly	___ e l ___ y
June	J ___ ___ e
January	___ ___ a ___ u ___ r ___

20

Activity Sheet

Write five words that begin with letter Jj

1. _____

2. _____

3. _____

4. _____

5. _____

Activity Sheet

Write these words in ABC order

jelly   1. _____

January   2. _____

jeans   3. _____

juggler   4. _____

July   5. _____

jacket   6. _____

June   7. _____

jello   8. _____

juice   9. _____

jam   10. _____

22

Activity Sheet

Write 2 sentences using one upper case "J" word and one lower case "j" word.

1. _____

   _____.

2. _____

   _____.

Activity Sheet

Write 3 to five 5 words that begin with the first letter of <u>your first name</u>.

1. _____

2. _____

3. _____

4. _____

5. _____

Added Skills

Learners and readers take another look,

at the extra pages added in this book.

These activities will take a different turn,

continue to read and enjoy as you learn.

They also are great skilful learning tools,

to use in homes, with friends or in schools.

Readers and learners, I won't hesitate,

to tell of another way that you can communicate.

The American Sign Language is really swell,

it is the same even when you say, "A-S-L."

The American Sign Language is an all time treasure,

and is included for your learning pleasure.

The objective is for scholars to fully understand, that communication can be done by mouth or with hands.

Be persistent and untiring with the understanding, that time with this method can be somewhat demanding.

So, readers are you ready for this next part? Then let's learn from the ASL Alphabet and Numbers Chart.

Start with the task of learning with your hands, as your knowledge of American Sign Language grows and expands.

Additional Learning Tasks

The following pictured pages are from The American Society for Deaf Children.

These great teaching and learning tools, which are: the American Sign Language (ASL) Alphabet and Numbers Charts can open new avenues of cognitive awareness for all learners.

Hopefully, scholars will begin practicing the use of the American Sign Language (ASL) Alphabet and Numbers. After which, scholars should be able to progress on from fingerspelling to becoming proficient, over time in using the actual ASL (signing) skills.

This unique method of communication can be beneficial for all concerned: the hard of hearing and deaf population as well as the hearing population.

Similarities yet differences in some numbers and alphabet,

will be explained so you will not forget.

The Standard English alphabet which we use each day,

and the ASL's are similar, but in a different way.

One similarity but difference that you should know,

starts with the number "zero (0)" and the alphabet "O."

Another difference, but likeness that you will see,

is with the number "four (4)" and the alphabet "B."

As you notice these two, I'm sure you'll agree,
there's a similarity with the number "one (1)" and
alphabet "D."

Here are three comparisons that are meant for
you,
they're alphabet "U" and "V" along with the number
"two (2)."

Another unique observation and similarity, is with
alphabet "W" and the number
"three (3)."

Tackle these tasks together and when you are
done,
hopefully you'll see that effective learning is
important and fun!

ASL Alphabet

Find more ASL resources at www.deafchildren.org

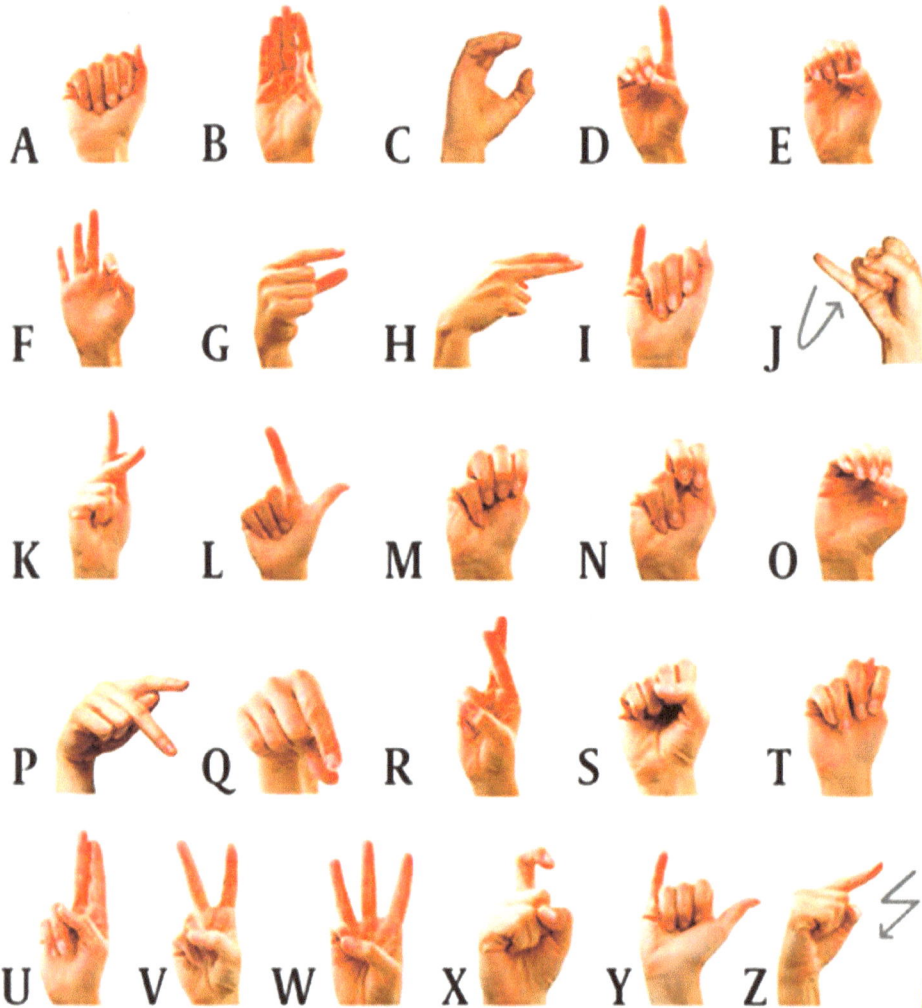

A   B   C   D   E

F   G   H   I   J

K   L   M   N   O

P   Q   R   S   T

U   V   W   X   Y   Z

American Society for Deaf Children

ASL Numbers

Find more ASL resources at www.deafchildren.org

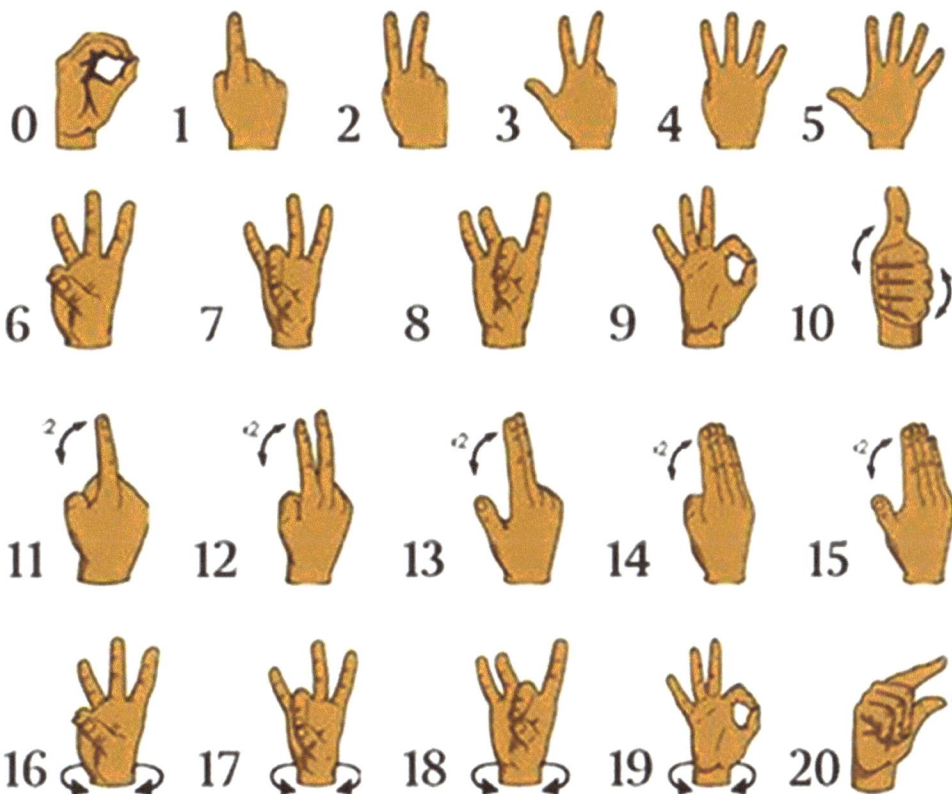

Note For the numbers 1-5, it's best practice to sign them with your palm facing your body. However, it's acceptable to sign 1-5 with your palm facing forward (as shown here) if you are emphasizing the number, signing a two-digit number such as 64, or if you're signing a series of numbers such as a phone number time, date, or age.

American Society for Deaf Children

Learning the alphabet and numbers is where you should start,
then advance to fingerspelling which is the progressive part.

You can practice fingerspelling, and you can even rehearse,
but you'll need to master the alphabet and the numbers first.

ASL upper and lower case alphabet are formed the same,
put this skill to work and fingerspell your name.

With these skilful activities, you should do just fine,
as you advance from fingerspelling to learning how to sign.

If you fingerspell or sign this is what you can do,
talk to the hard of hearing and the deaf population too.

It's a unique way to communicate without a spoken word,
when expressed correctly it is as if they've heard.

Some people will see exactly what you have to say,
when you talk to them in this non-verbal way.

Using American Sign Language can be in high demands,
when you progress to signing; communicating with your hands.

Once proficient in this method please do not forget, the unique American Sign Language Numbers and (ASL) Alphabet!

You can study during the day you can practice during the night,
you can learn more about signing when you visit this great website:

www.deafchildren.org

Skillful Suggestions

Listed below are a few suggestions to use upon the completion of this story. Incorporate these and other skills according to the reader's functioning abilities.

1. Ask learner to say or point to the title of this book.

2. Ask learner to say or point to the author's and/or illustrator's names.

3. Ask learner to name the character/juggler in this story.

4. Ask learner what letter of the alphabet is this character using?

5. Ask learner how many Jj things did this character juggle in all?

6. Ask learner to name/point to as many of these "Jj" items as possible (with or without assistance).

Skillful Suggestions

Listed below are a few suggestions to use upon the completion of this story. Incorporate these and other skills according to the reader's functioning abilities.

7. Ask learner how many upper case J and how many lower case j words are in the Words to Know List?

8. Ask learner what communication method is introduced in this book? (American Sign Language (ASL) Alphabet/Numbers Chart).

9. Teach the entire American Sign Language (ASL) Alphabet as well as the ASL Numbers.

10. While teaching the ASL Alphabet and Numbers, keep in mind that this can become time consuming.

Skillful Suggestions

Listed below are a few suggestions to use upon the completion of this story. Incorporate these and other skills according to the reader's functioning abilities.

11. Upon learning the ASL Alphabet and Numbers, ask learner to fingerspell his/her name and/ or count the letters in her/his name using ASL method.

12. Incorporate various learning activities involving fingerspelling and/or counting using the ASL method.

13. Ask learner to fingerspell and/or count the words on the "Words to Know List" using the ASL method.

14. Include these ASL lesson according to learner's individual abilities.

15. Upon mastery, present the AWARD!

AWARD

(Learner's Name)

Has shown some knowledge/understanding in learning the American Sign Language (ASL) Alphabet/Numbers per this teaching session.

_____ _____
(Adult Guide's Signature)   Date

GREAT JOB to ALL!! (Guides/Learners)

Aa Ss Ll

Acknowledgements

~ Extreme thanks to Gaurav Bhatnagar with ePublishingeXperts for his continued Awesome Illustrations and Wonderful Publishing Expertise!!

~ Exceptional thanks to the American Society for Deaf Children; www.deafchildren.org Cheri Dowling, Executive Director for giving me permission to use their American Sign Language (ASL) Alphabet Chart and their American Sign Language (ASL) Numbers Chart for the enhancement of this book.

~ Extraordinary thanks to my niece, Tina Lewis (teacher/author) for her great work.

~ Exclusive thanks to Delesilyn Elston, Retired Teacher of the Deaf.

Remember Royal, Ready Readers:

There is a need;
You need to read!

Wherever you are;
Be a S.T.A.R.
(Stand Tall And Read)

Remember the drill;
Always keep it R.E.A.L.
(Read Enjoy And Learn)

Once you're a skilled reader,
you can take center stage,

with the class of other scholars who know
how to R.A.G.E.
(Read Above Grade Expectation)

Author's Information/Published Books on Amazon

Email: morepsplease@gmail.com
Face Book: Fannie Lewis Barnes
Amazon.com: Books by Fannie Lewis Barnes

~ <u>I Must Read</u> - Curriculum/Common Core Standards Based Material, (Alphabets A-Z, pictures, long/short vowels, simple sentences, instructions)

~ <u>Reading As I Learn (R.A.I.L.)</u> – Counting 1-10, number words, colors, color words, pictures

~ <u>Ray and Mae (Bringing Smiles)</u> – Best Bunny Buddies making everyone and everything happy when they are near

~ <u>My Little Friends</u> – (Different baby animals)

~ <u>Let's Stick Together</u> – (Friends sticking together)

~ <u>Once Upon A Time</u> - (A story of talking insects)

~ <u>I Like Likeable Things</u> – (A story of various things that different children like to do and like to eat)

~ <u>A Fish Named Dowg</u> – (A story of how this fish acquired its name and things done for the friends, E'Rock and Spike)

<u>Note:</u> All books include Worksheets and Skill Suggestions.

Jason (son) enjoyed having various children stories read to him when he was very young; hopefully he will enjoy this book even more since it is penned with him in mind.

This story tells of things that Jason likes to juggle, as long as they begin with the letter, "Jj," like the initial letter of his first name.

Included in the latter part of this book are communication tools for extra learning; namely, the American Sign Language (ASL) Alphabet and the (ASL) Numbers via the American Society for Deaf Children.

These skills are included in order to awaken other cognitive and learning interests in the hearing population of readers.

Becoming skilled in ASL can prove beneficial for all concerned: the hard of hearing and deaf population as well as the hearing population.

Aa Ss Ll

ISBN 978-1-7376571-8-7

9 781737 657187

www.ingramcontent.com/pod-product-compliance
Lightning Source LLC
LaVergne TN
LVHW072119070426
835511LV00002B/29

9 781737 657187